GRAPHIC HISTORY

The Sinking of the
TITANIC

by Matt Doeden
illustrated by Charles Barnett III
and Phil Miller

Consultant:
Norm Lewis
Canadian Titanic Society
Simcoe, Ontario

Capstone
PRESS

Mankato, Minnesota

Graphic Library is published by Capstone Press,
151 Good Counsel Drive, P.O. Box 669, Mankato, Minnesota 56002.
www.capstonepress.com

1 2 3 4 5 6 10 09 08 07 06 05

Library of Congress Cataloging-in-Publication Data
Doeden, Matt.
    The sinking of the Titanic / by Matt Doeden; illustrated by Charles Barnett III
    and Phil Miller.
    p. cm.—(Graphic library. Graphic history.)
    Includes bibliographical references and index.
    ISBN 0-7368-3834-1 (hardcover)
    ISBN 0-7368-5247-6 (paperback)
    1. Titanic (Steamship)—Juvenile literature. 2. Shipwrecks—North Atlantic Ocean—Juvenile
literature. I. Barnett, Charles, III and Phil Miller, ill. II. Title. III. Series.
G530.T6D64 2005
910'.9163'4—dc22   2004015585

Summary: The story of the 1912 sinking of the *Titanic* is told in a graphic-novel format.

Editor's note: Direct quotations from primary sources are indicated by a yellow background.

Direct quotations appear on the following pages:
Pages 11, 13, 15, 17, 18, 21, 26, from the American and British *Titanic* Inquiry transcripts
    (http://www.titanicinquiry.org)
Page 7, from a letter sent before the sinking (http://www.titanic-titanic.com)
Pages 9, 16, from the Marconi Corporation, Ice Warning Messages to and from *Titanic*
    (http://www.marconicalling.com)

Credits
Art Director and Storyboard Artist
Jason Knudson

Colorist
Brent Schoonover

Editor
Sarah L. Schuette

Acknowledgements
Capstone Press thanks Philip Charles
Crawford, Library Director, Essex High
School, Essex, Vermont, and columnist for
Knowledge Quest, for his assistance
in the preparation of this book.

Capstone Press thanks Charles Barnett III
and Phil Miller of Cavalier Graphics.

TABLE OF CONTENTS

Chapter 1

A GRAND VOYAGE BEGINS!

On April 10, 1912, the giant ocean liner *Titanic* floated in the harbor at Southampton, England. *Titanic* was the largest ship ever built at that time. It was as long as four city blocks and as tall as a ten-story building.

Newspapers reported that *Titanic* was practically an unsinkable ship. In the event of an accident, the ship had watertight compartments to keep it afloat. People believed that these compartments and other features of the ship made *Titanic* the safest ship ever built.

Captain Edward J. Smith had sailed the seas for more than 20 years. Smith would command *Titanic*'s first trip across the Atlantic Ocean to New York City.

Easy, now. This is my last voyage as a captain and I want everything to go smoothly.

Standing on the bridge, Captain Smith gave the order, and *Titanic* slowly pulled out of the harbor. Well-wishers lined the dock, waving farewell to the famous ship and its 2,200 passengers and crew.

Say hello to New York for us!

Safe voyage!

First-class passengers traveled in luxury. Millionaires such as Benjamin Guggenheim, Molly Brown, and John Astor danced in sparkling ballrooms, ate in elaborate dining rooms, and slept in beautiful brand-new cabins.

This ship is a marvel.

Fantastic!

It ought to be, for the price of a ticket.

Molly Brown toured Europe and stayed with the Astors before returning to America on *Titanic*. At home, Molly's husband was a very successful miner. Molly used her money to help people in need.

On the lower decks, second-class and third-class passengers explored the ship. Even the lower areas of the ship were impressive.

Joseph and Juliette Laroche sailed with their young family. Like many passengers, Juliette was eager to write letters to family back home.

Dear Dad,
We boarded the *Titanic* last evening at 7:00. The boat set out when we were eating and we could not believe she was moving. The sea is very smooth, the weather is wonderful. If you could see how big this ship is!

The sea is so calm.

What a beautiful evening.

The great ship made excellent time as it crossed the cold North Atlantic. Passengers walked along *Titanic's* decks and enjoyed perfect weather. They danced to the ship's band in the ballroom.

Titanic's passengers and crew were unaware of the trouble ahead.

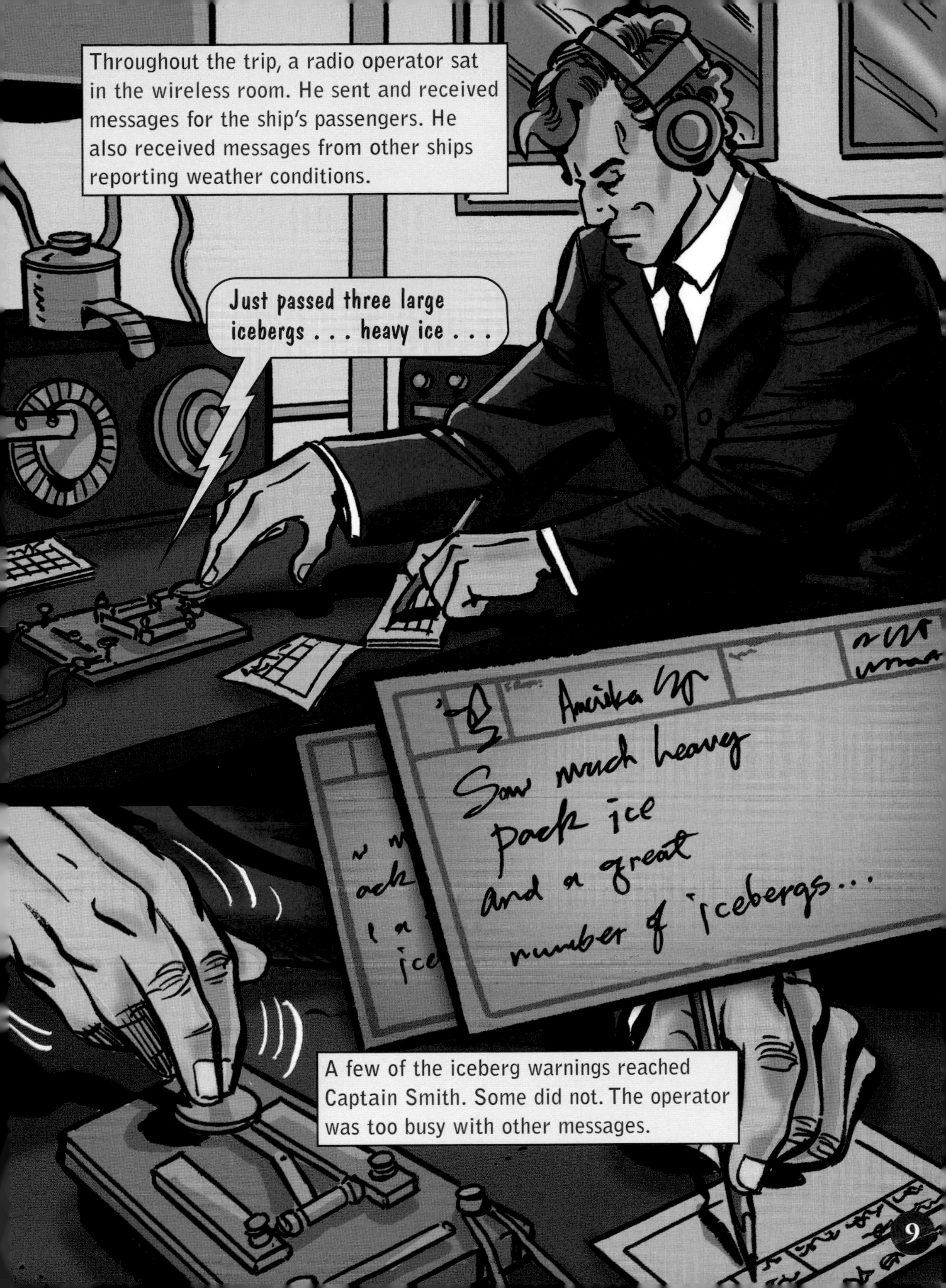
Throughout the trip, a radio operator sat in the wireless room. He sent and received messages for the ship's passengers. He also received messages from other ships reporting weather conditions.
Just passed three large icebergs . . . heavy ice . . .
Amerika
Saw much heavy pack ice and a great number of icebergs...
A few of the iceberg warnings reached Captain Smith. Some did not. The operator was too busy with other messages.

Chapter 2
COLLISION

Shortly before midnight on April 14, Frederick Fleet and another crew member were on watch duty in *Titanic's* crow's nest. The water was calm. The ship moved quickly through the cool night.

It's so dark tonight. I wish I had binoculars.

Fleet suddenly spotted a low, dark shape floating directly in the ship's path.

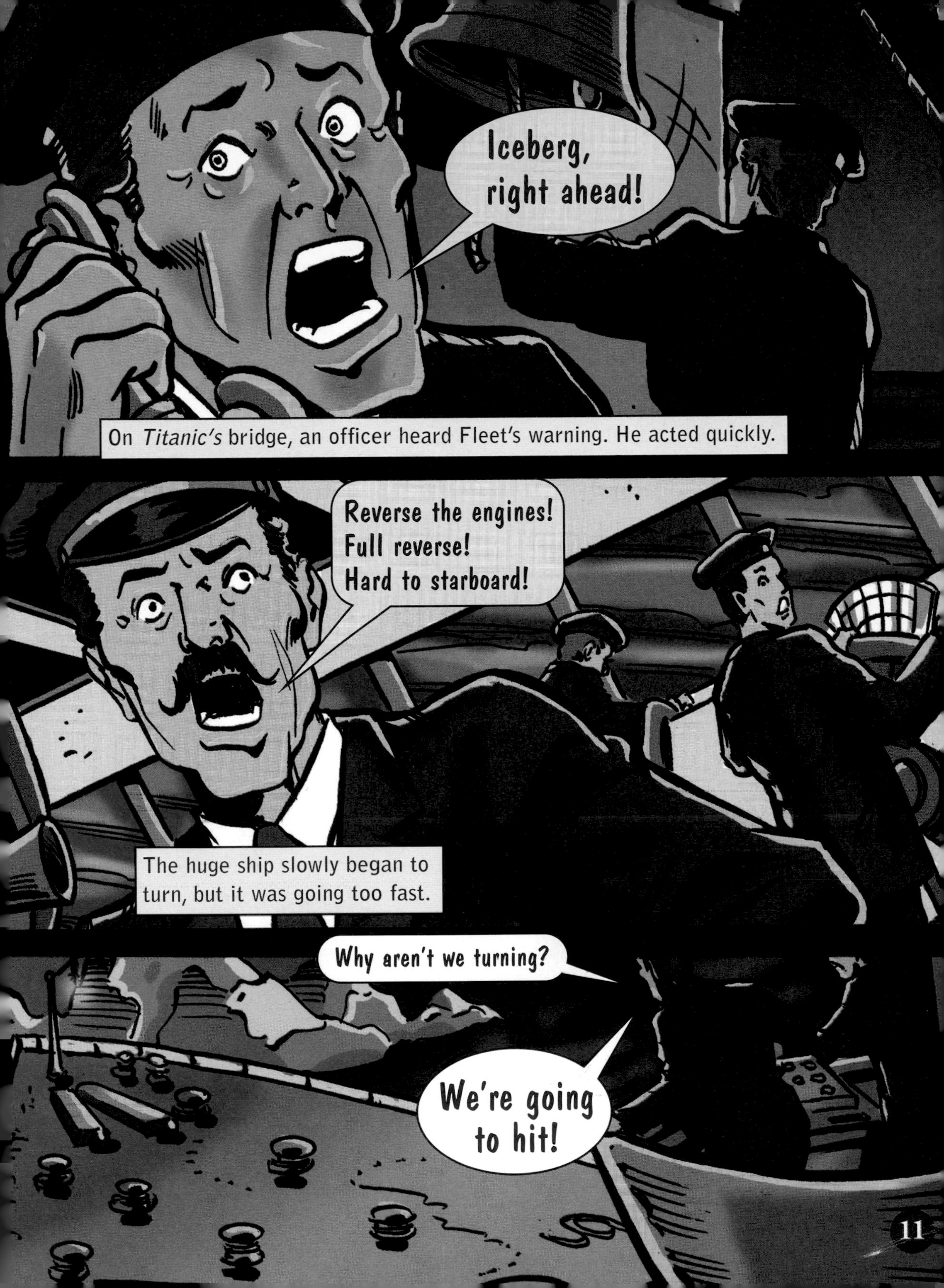
Iceberg, right ahead!
On *Titanic's* bridge, an officer heard Fleet's warning. He acted quickly.
Reverse the engines! Full reverse! Hard to starboard!
The huge ship slowly began to turn, but it was going too fast.
Why aren't we turning?
We're going to hit!

SCREECH!!

Metal tore as the iceberg ripped through the hull. Instantly, thousands of gallons of water poured into the lower areas of the ship.

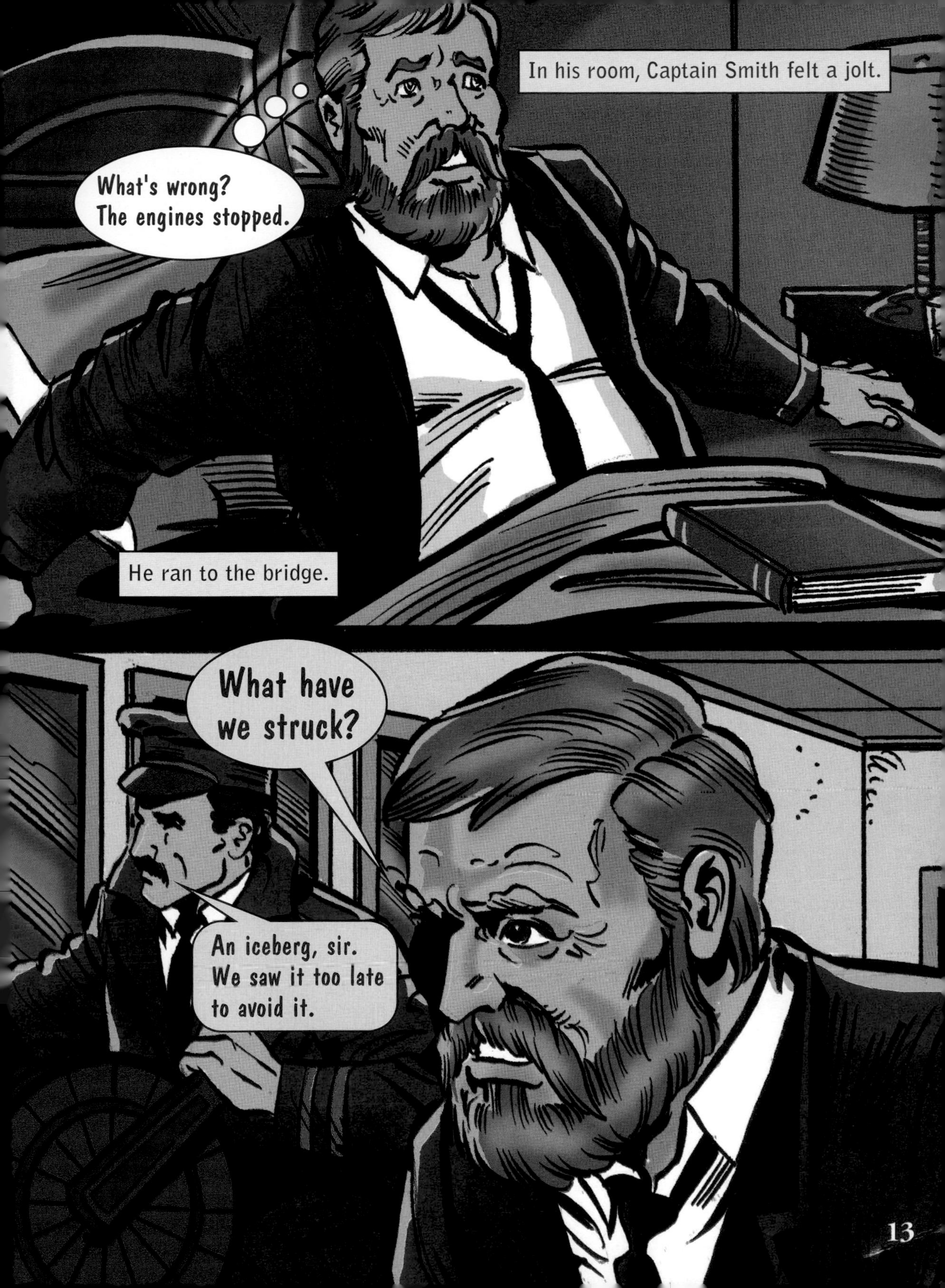
In his room, Captain Smith felt a jolt.
What's wrong? The engines stopped.
He ran to the bridge.
What have we struck?
An iceberg, sir. We saw it too late to avoid it.

Chapter 3

TITANIC'S FATE IS SEALED

Minutes later, Thomas Andrews, *Titanic's* chief designer, toured the lower decks with Captain Smith.

How bad is it, Mr. Andrews?

Very bad, I'm afraid. The iceberg has ripped many holes. The water's coming in too fast. *Titanic* cannot survive.

How long do we have?

An hour and a half. Possibly two.

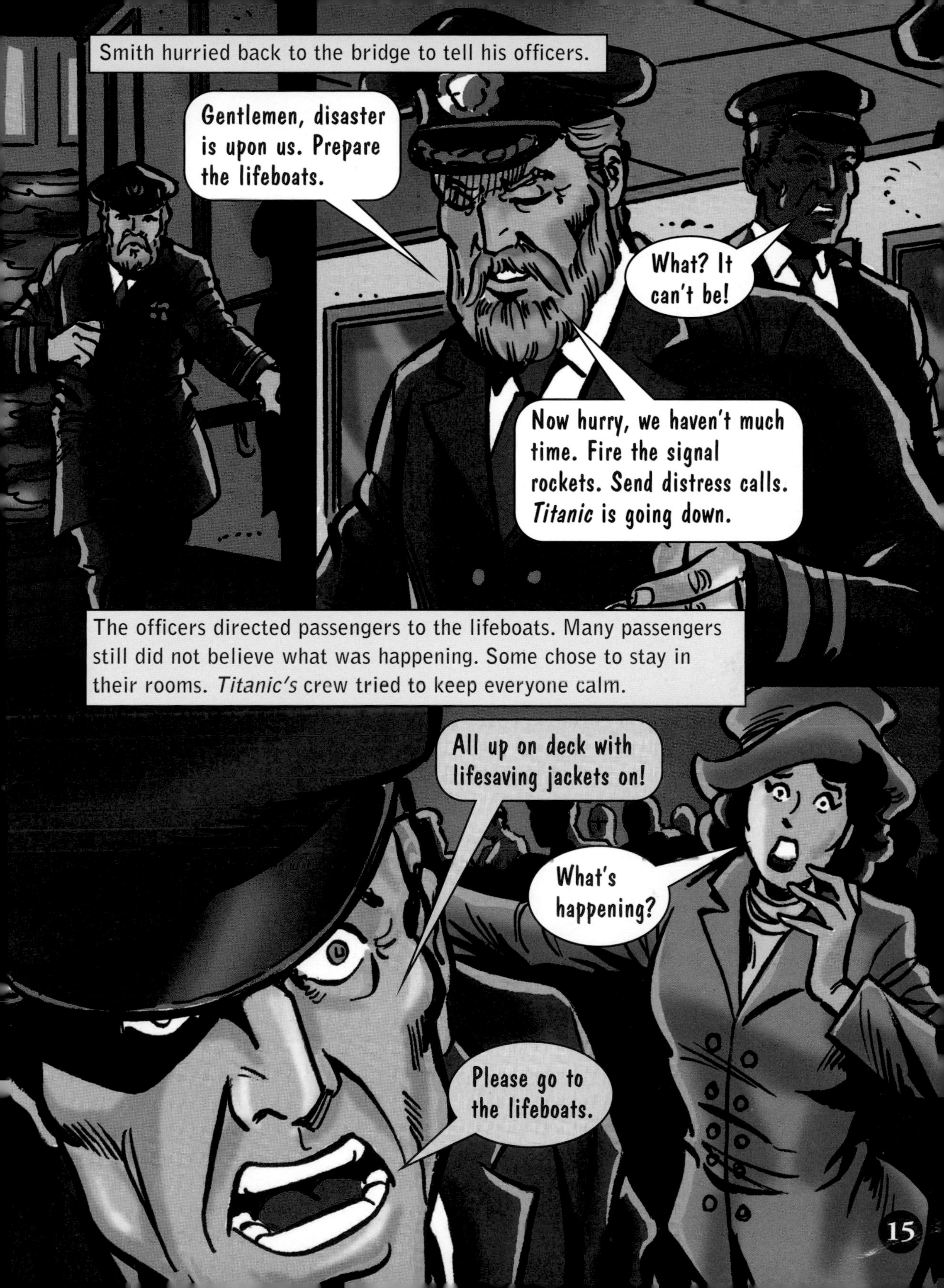
Smith hurried back to the bridge to tell his officers.
Gentlemen, disaster is upon us. Prepare the lifeboats.
What? It can't be!
Now hurry, we haven't much time. Fire the signal rockets. Send distress calls. *Titanic* is going down.
The officers directed passengers to the lifeboats. Many passengers still did not believe what was happening. Some chose to stay in their rooms. *Titanic's* crew tried to keep everyone calm.
All up on deck with lifesaving jackets on!
What's happening?
Please go to the lifeboats.

Immediately, the radio operators sent distress calls, hoping another ship in the area could help.

Have struck iceberg and sinking. We require immediate assistance.

The *Californian* was only 10 miles away from *Titanic*. Its radio operator had already gone to sleep. Other crew members noticed flashes of light in the night sky.

On board the *Californian*, an officer woke the captain.

Captain, we've spotted signal rockets in the distance. It might be a distress signal.

It's probably just fireworks. Don't worry about it.

The *Carpathia* was 58 miles, or about four hours, away from *Titanic*.

The radio operator on the *Carpathia* was still awake and received *Titanic's* distress call. He quickly sent the message to Captain A. H. Rostron.

Captain, *Titanic* is going down and is requesting help.

Go! Go as fast as we can to get there!

We'll never make it in time.

Wake the crew.

Meanwhile, *Titanic* was sinking fast.

Women and children first!

Officers started loading passengers onto lifeboats. *Titanic* had only enough lifeboats for about 1,200 people. In the rush, many lifeboats were lowered with empty spaces.

Families were split up. As the women and children boarded the boats first, most men waited behind. Some did not realize they would never see their loved ones again.

Chapter 4

THE END OF *TITANIC*

The lifeboats were lowered quickly. More than 1,500 people remained on the ship with no hope of being saved. Some jumped into the freezing water.

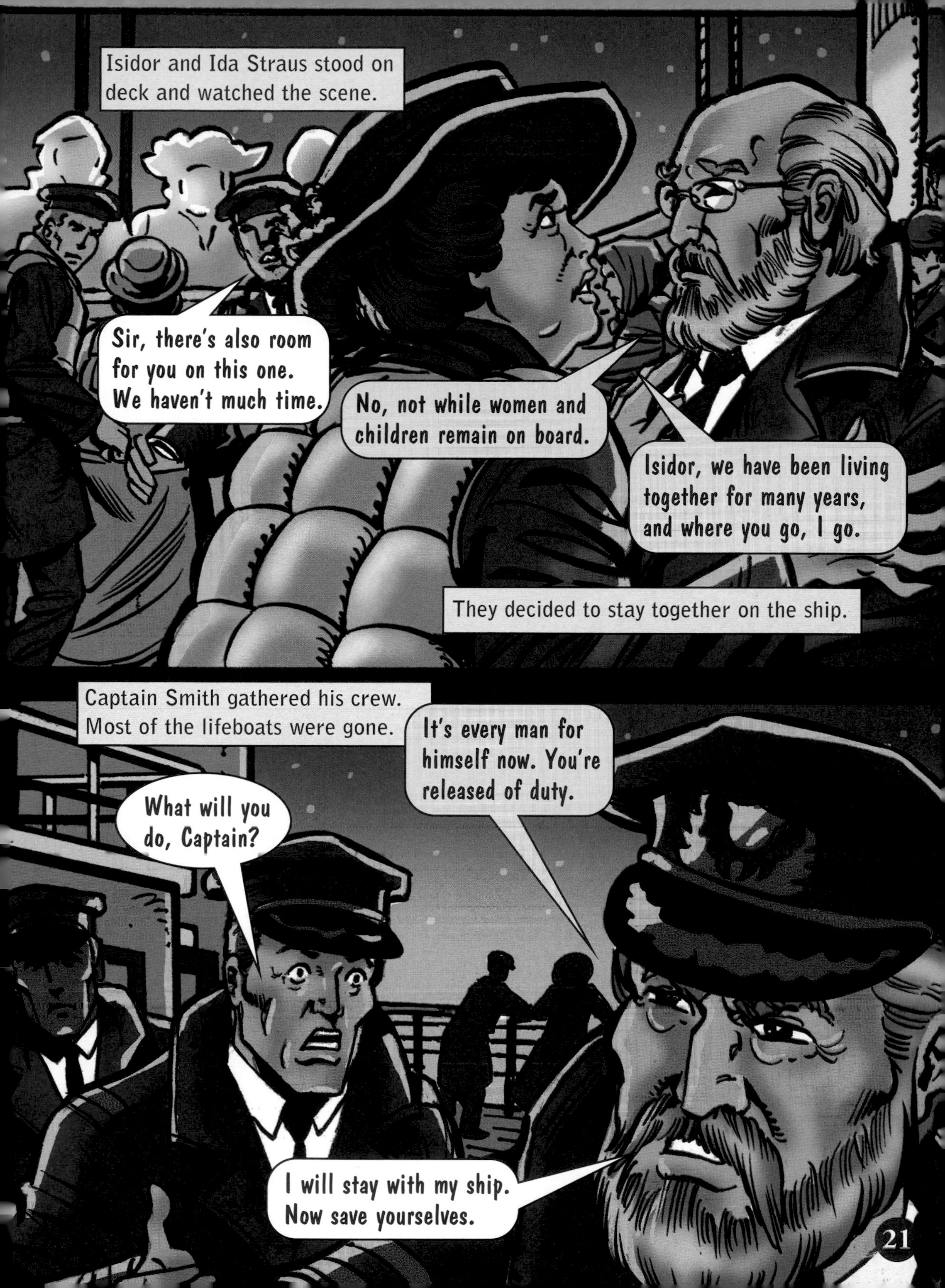
Isidor and Ida Straus stood on deck and watched the scene.
Sir, there's also room for you on this one. We haven't much time.
No, not while women and children remain on board.
Isidor, we have been living together for many years, and where you go, I go.
They decided to stay together on the ship.
Captain Smith gathered his crew. Most of the lifeboats were gone.
It's every man for himself now. You're released of duty.
What will you do, Captain?
I will stay with my ship. Now save yourselves.

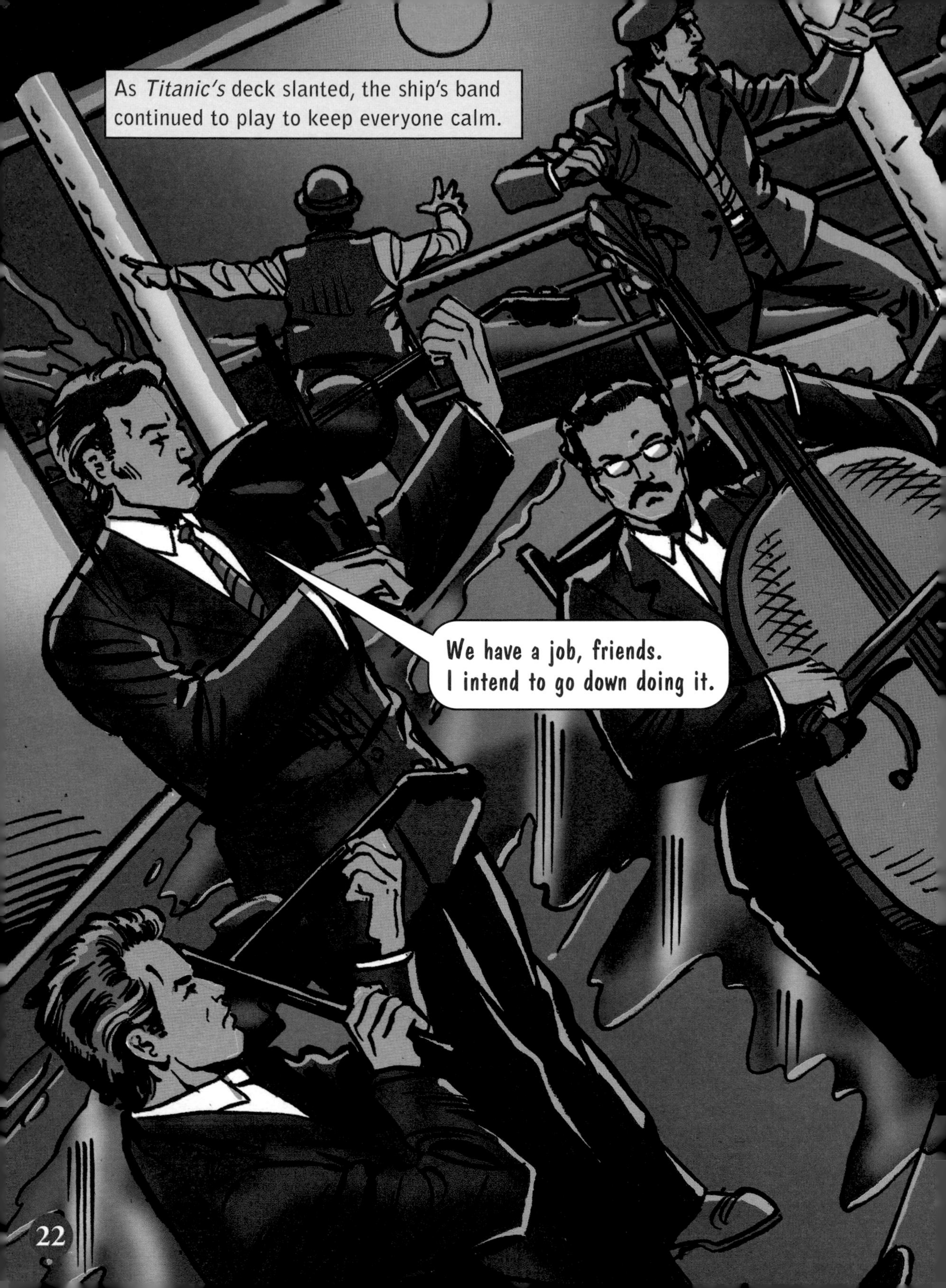
As *Titanic's* deck slanted, the ship's band continued to play to keep everyone calm.
We have a job, friends. I intend to go down doing it.

At 2:17 in the morning, *Titanic's* stern raised out of the water. Its giant propellers hung in the air. *Titanic's* lights flickered and went out.

The ship split in half. The front half quickly sank.

CRAACK!

23

The stern remained above the surface for a moment. Then *Titanic* slipped into the ocean.

Keep rowing away from the ship!

The great ship was gone. In the darkness, people clung to wreckage and floated in the freezing water. Survivors in lifeboats heard their cries for help.

Someone, help us!

It's so cold.

In one lifeboat, Molly Brown argued with the officer in charge of the boat.

We have to go back! We have more room!

No, we can't. They'll swamp the boat and kill us all. There's nothing we can do.

Finally, about two hours after *Titanic* sank, the *Carpathia* reached the scene. Survivors in lifeboats rowed to meet the ship.

Aboard the *Carpathia*, Captain Rostron was saddened.

We're too late.

Get to the lifeboats. Save everyone you can.

Survivors climbed rope ladders to the *Carpathia*. The crew did what it could to comfort them.

It'll be all right.

The *Carpathia* carried only 705 survivors to New York City. Thousands of people met the ship as it docked, searching for friends or family members. Most learned the worst.

More than 1,500 people died in the cold waters of the North Atlantic. The sinking of *Titanic* was one of the most deadly disasters of its time.

★ *Titanic* was owned by the White Star Line steamship company. Construction of the ship began in 1909 in Belfast, Ireland. It took two years for 3,000 workers to build the ship.

★ Fully loaded, *Titanic* weighed more than 50,000 tons (45 metric tons).

★ *Titanic* cost about $7 million to build. Today, it would cost about $400 million.

★ First-class passengers paid about $4,350 to sail on *Titanic*. Second-class passengers paid about $65, and third-class passengers paid about $35.

★ *Titanic*'s maiden voyage began on April 10, 1912. After hitting the iceberg around 11:40 at night on April 14, *Titanic* sank around 2:20 in the morning on April 15.

★ Due to a last-minute crew change, no one noticed until the voyage began that the binoculars were missing from the crow's nest. Some people believe that if Frederick Fleet had used binoculars, *Titanic* could have steered clear of the iceberg. Others believe the low quality of the binoculars would not have helped Fleet see the iceberg any sooner.

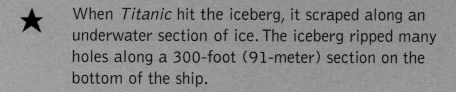 When *Titanic* hit the iceberg, it scraped along an underwater section of ice. The iceberg ripped many holes along a 300-foot (91-meter) section on the bottom of the ship.

Titanic carried 20 lifeboats. To save all passengers and crew on board, *Titanic* would have needed 48 lifeboats.

The exact location of *Titanic*'s wreckage was unknown for 73 years. Then in 1985, Dr. Robert Ballard led a team of explorers to find *Titanic*. The team finally found the great sunken ship 2.5 miles (4 kilometers) beneath the surface of the Atlantic Ocean.

GLOSSARY

bridge (BRIJ)—the control center of a ship

crow's nest (KROHZ NEST)—a lookout post located high above the ship

distress signal (diss-TRESS SIG-nuhl)—a call for help from a ship; operators sent distress signals from the wireless room.

harbor (HAR-bur)—a place where ships load and unload passengers and cargo

hull (HUHL)—the frame or body of a ship

propeller (pruh-PEL-ur)—a set of rotating blades that provides the force to move a ship through water

starboard (STAR-burd)—the right-hand side of a ship

stern (STERN)—the back half of a ship

INTERNET SITES

FactHound offers a safe, fun way to find Internet sites related to this book. All of the sites on FactHound have been researched by our staff.

Here's how:

1. Visit *www.facthound.com*
2. Type in this special code **0736838341** for age-appropriate sites. Or enter a search word related to this book for a more general search.
3. Click on the **Fetch It** button.

FactHound will fetch the best sites for you!

READ MORE

Deady, Kathleen W. *The Titanic: The Tragedy at Sea.* Disaster! Mankato, Minn.: Capstone Press, 2003.

Harmon, Daniel E. *The Titanic.* Great Disasters, Reforms, and Ramifications. Philadelphia: Chelsea House, 2001.

Matsen, Bradford. *The Incredible Quest to Find the Titanic.* Incredible Deep-sea Adventures. Berkeley Heights, N.J.: Enslow, 2003.

BIBLIOGRAPHY

Ballard, Robert D. *The Discovery of the Titanic.* New York: Warner Books, 1987.

Gardiner, Robin. *The History of the White Star Line.* Hersham: Ian Allan, 2001.

The Marconi Corporation, Ice Warning Messages, http://www.marconicalling.com.

Titanic Inquiry Project, American and British Inquiry Transcripts http://www.titanicinquiry.com.

Walter, Lord. *A Night to Remember.* New York: Holt, Rinehart, & Winston, 1976.

Wels, Susan. *Titanic: Legacy of the World's Greatest Ocean Liner.* Alexandria, Va.: Time-Life Books, 1997.

INDEX